AF378580

# GOODBYE COVENT GARDEN

Ena Bodin

Oxford Illustrated Press 1975

Set in Futura Book by Ace Engravers
Film supplied by EAGLE LITHO
Printed in the City of Oxford by Blackwells
Bound by Henry Brooks, and Kemp Hall, Oxford

Oxford Illustrated Press, Shelley Close, Risinghurst, Oxford

# Introduction

by The Marquess of Tavistock

I have always been fascinated by the history of Covent Garden Market which was owned and developed by my ancestors for 350 years.

The market originally began in the Middle Ages, when the Abbots of Westminster who owned some pasture land and orchards, known as the 'Convent Garden', began to sell their surplus production to the citizens of London. As the city grew, the population created a demand for ever-increasing quantities of fresh fruit and vegetables. Farmers from the surrounding country-side began to bring their crops to the wall of the Convent Garden for sale and gradually an informal market became established.

Upon the dissolution of the monasteries by Henry VIII the land became the property of the Crown, and remained so until 1552 when King Edward VI granted the walled garden of three acres and the adjoining seven acre field (Long Acre) to my ancestor John Russell, 1st Earl of Bedford. This land was leased to tenant farmers for nearly 100 years until the 4th Earl of Bedford decided to make the Covent Garden estate more profitable.

The Earl was a shrewd business man and planned to build houses on the estate which could be leased at good rents to 'Gents and men of ability'. Building began in 1631 under the direction of Isaac de Caux, an architect and garden designer. However, it was in fact Inigo Jones who actually designed the overall scheme, which was the first development outside the city boundaries to be planned so formally (a piazza in the Italian style), and was the first and finest of London's residential squares.

The Earl also commissioned St Pauls Church. It is said that he once told Inigo Jones that he could scarcely afford a barn, let alone a church, to which Jones replied 'Then my Lord you shall have the handsomest barn in England'.

The Piazza with its fine portico walks quickly became very popular and in 1662 Samuel Pepys described the square as a 'great resort of gallants'. About the same time a formal market began and the 5th Earl built shops along the garden wall of Bedford House.

Covent Garden received royal recognition 12 May 1670 when Charles II granted the Earl a charter 'to hold for ever a market in the Piazza on every day of the year except sundays and Christmas Day for the buying and selling of all manner of fruit, flowers, root and herbs...'

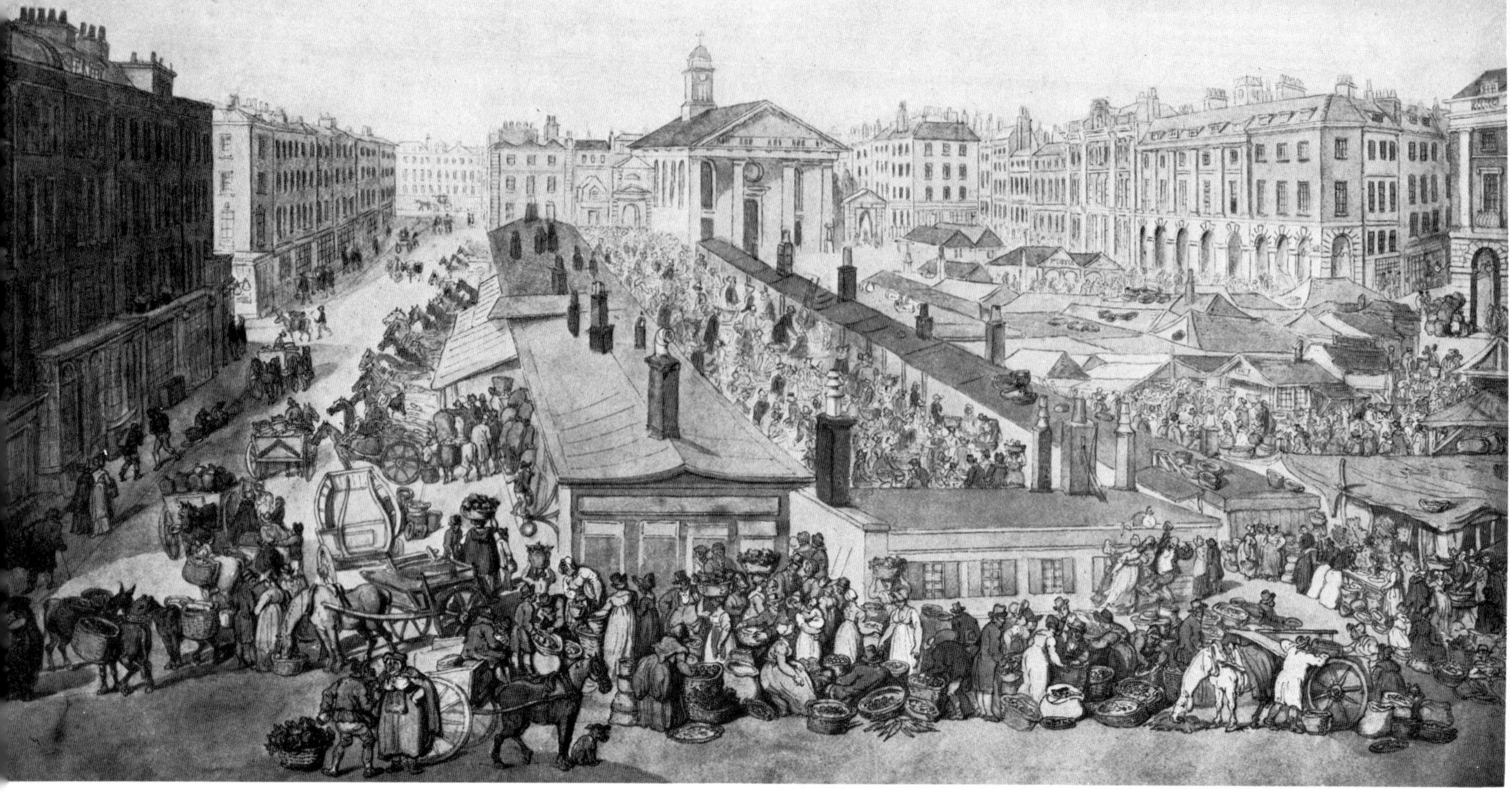

*Watercolour: Thomas Rowlandson* *Woburn Abbey Collection*
Covent Garden in 1812 showing St Paul's Church and the piazza designed by Inigo Jones, and the development of the flourishing market in the centre of the square.

*Watercolour: artist unknown* *Woburn Abbey Collection*
By 1828 the market with its ever-increasing number of huts and stalls had become unmanageable. To improve this situation, the 6th Earl of Bedford commissioned the Dedicated Market to be built in the centre of the square.

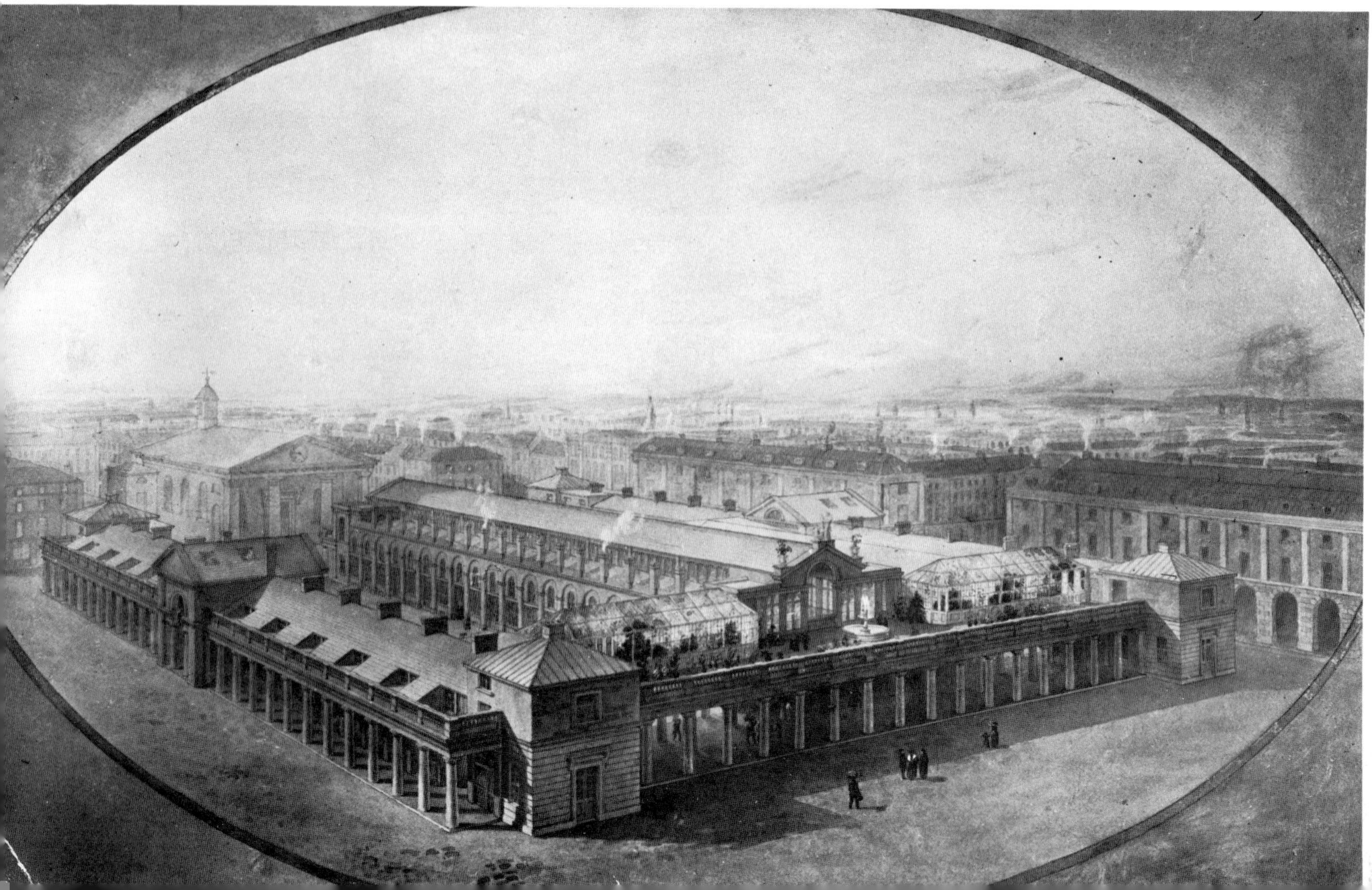

Trading flourished and the market quickly spread into the centre of the square. By the end of the eighteenth century it had become 'the greatest market in England for herbs, fruit and flowers.' With success came other problems however; people had begun to complain about the noise and congestion caused by the market. The situation eventually resulted in an Act being passed by parliament in 1828 giving the Earl statuory power to demolish the existing buildings and erect a new market. Between 1828 and 1830, the Dedicated Market was built based on the designs of the architect Charles Fowler. Each warehouse had a cellar and upper floor for storage and the walkway between the 'shops' was wide enough for temporary stalls. The resulting market was both efficient and popular.

By 1880 however the extensive use of the market had again over-reached its facilities and a prolonged attack was mounted by Punch under the heading of 'Mud Salad Market' in which the market was described as 'a disgrace to London, a special disgrace to his Grace of Mudsford and about the greatest nuisance ever permitted in a great City of Nuisance'. The Duke tried to sell the market to the Metropolitan Board of Works in 1883 but they turned the offer down. The City Corporation also refused the offer but finally in 1914 the property was sold to the Beecham Estate and Pills Ltd.

The Market passed through several hands before the Covent Garden Market Act of 1961 established the Covent Garden Market Authorities and vested in them the market and some of the surrounding land. On 9 April 1964, the Authority recommended to the Minister of Agriculture, Fisheries and Food that a new market should be built at Nine Elms approximately two miles from the original site.

The market prior to the move, had an annual turnover of approximately £75 million and some 4-5000 people bought sold and carried produce through it daily.

The need for its move across the Thames to Nine Elms was unquestionable, but it has left in its wake a sadness for those who knew and loved the atmosphere of the Garden. The host of characters and their legends will undoubtedly continue to exist behind the closed doors of the new and efficient market, but no longer will London vibrate from the unique mixture of opera goers, office workers, tourists and porters that was…

COVENT GARDEN

SAINT PAUL'S CHURCH
COVENT GARDEN
built by Inigo Jones 1633

St. Paul's Church from the site of the original Convent Garden

22.30 at the Royal Opera House

Strolling through the Dedicated Market

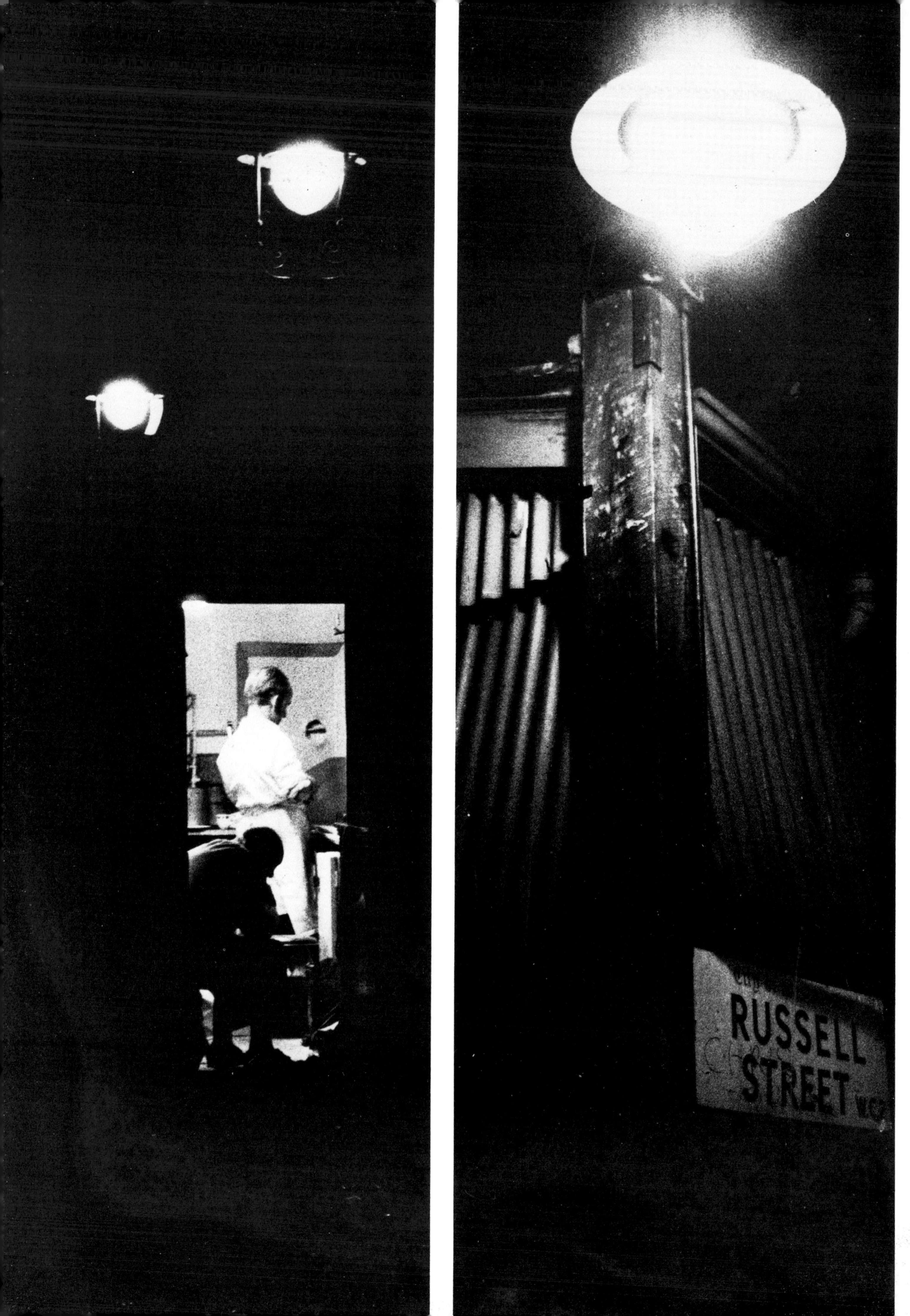
RUSSELL
STREET W.C.

Midnight: the market begins

BARNETT EMANUEL LTD
COMMISION SALESMEN
GB
XNJ
353J

WOO

A. COOPER & SONS
TRANSPORT Ld
45. BEDFORD RD.
SANDY, BEDS.
Phone

COVIAL
COVIAL
COVIAL
COVIAL
COVIAL
COVIAL
COVIAL
COVIAL
COVIAL
OGEN
OF ISRAEL
OF ISRAEL
OF ISRAEL

4.30: the buying starts

FLOWERS
Chrysanthemums
Fresh Fl*wers

5.00: the pubs open

The Opera House at sunrise

31 UPPER HIGH ST
ELSOM
YES, BUGNER
v. McALINDEN
HERMANOS
COCA

THIS TOILET
IS FOR THE USE O
MARKET WORKER
ONLY.
NO LOITERIN

WN & PACKED BY
TREMAIN & SONS
PEAR

CASTELLA
Beer festival

PERFECTION in Pot Plants.
EVANS
POT PLANTS

BANANA'S) LTD
MAJOR BROS
SKI TRIPS
CHRISTMAS
& NEW YEAR
HIGH BALL
HIGH BALL
HIGH BALL
HIGH BALL
HIGH BALL
STOP
CROWN & ANCHOR
COMMER
WPD
390G

KEMBLES HEAD
Theatre Bar
SALOON
SALOON
WATNEYS

WHITBREAD
FLORAL ST.
NAG'S HEAD
WHITBREAD
Nag
SALOON BAR
RESTAURANT
COVE
SALOON BAR
SALOON BAR
THE
NAG'S HEAD
LYW
662D

BALDWINS
COVER...Y
har
F. ALLEN

ULAGE
XTP 884
GROVURA
RAVENNA
GROVURA
RAVENNA

Parking is always a problem

White Lion

FRUITSALES LTD.
FRUITSALES LTD.
THE WHITE SERVICE

The market is almost over as commuters hurry to work

GOOD NEIGHBOURS DAY
SUNDAY 9th JUNE

BRITISH PRODUCE
TOMATOES
GUERNSEY TOMS
BRITISH PRODUCE
TOMATOES
GUERNSEY TOMS
GUERNSEY TOMS
REPUBLIC OF SOUTH AFRICA

Ciruelas
5 K
Ciruelas
9
9

Fifty years ago fruit was sold in baskets
and transport was the horse and cart.
All that has changed, but the buildings
are still the same.

Covent
Garden
Information
Centre
N°3
M.R. BENNETT LTD.
MA

W.LEDGER

JOSEP

Vincent Foliage Ltd.
VINCENT
Fresh Flowers
FRESH FLOWERS

A.E.BURREE & SON
COLLIER

ENGLISH PRO

The market is over

Covent
Garden
Information
Centre
GLC

WESTERN AUSTRALIA
WESTERN AUSTRALIA
WESTERN AUSTRALIA

STUART LOW
CO. (ENFIELD) LTD.

tions

NO GOODS OR ARTICLE
MAY BE PLACED IN
FRONT OF THIS GATE
BY ORDER
G.A.F.SUTTON

H. G. WALKER LTD
T. J. POUPART.

The market is cleared ready for the move to Vauxhall

TULLY
156M
207N



Bullens
REMOVALS & STORAGE
CHAMBE
WC2

JOHNS

GROOM & GREENS

EDWARD H. LEWIS & SON LTD
EDWARD H. LEWIS & SON LTD

FAREWELL
TO
COVENT GARDEN

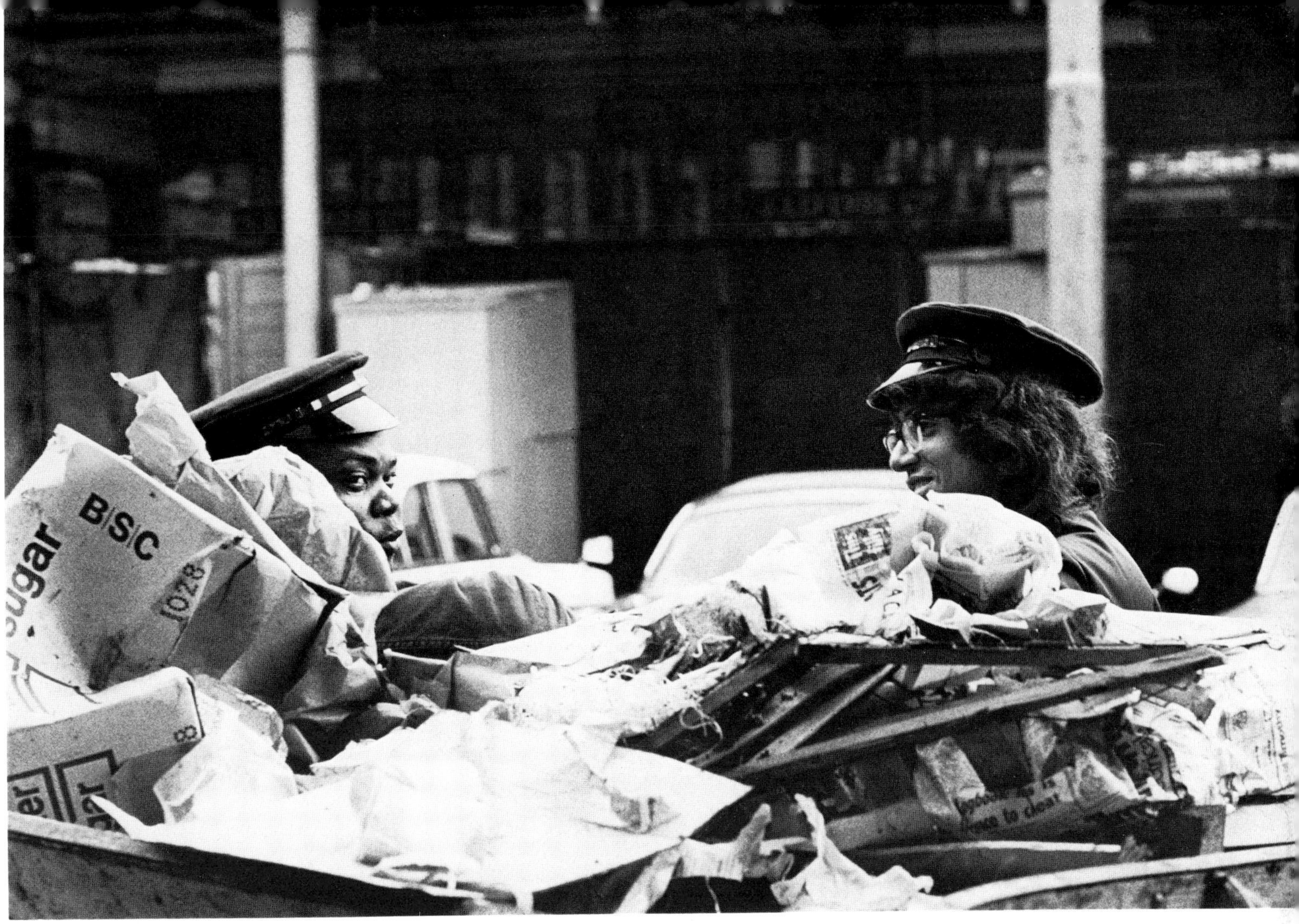

sugar
BSC
1028

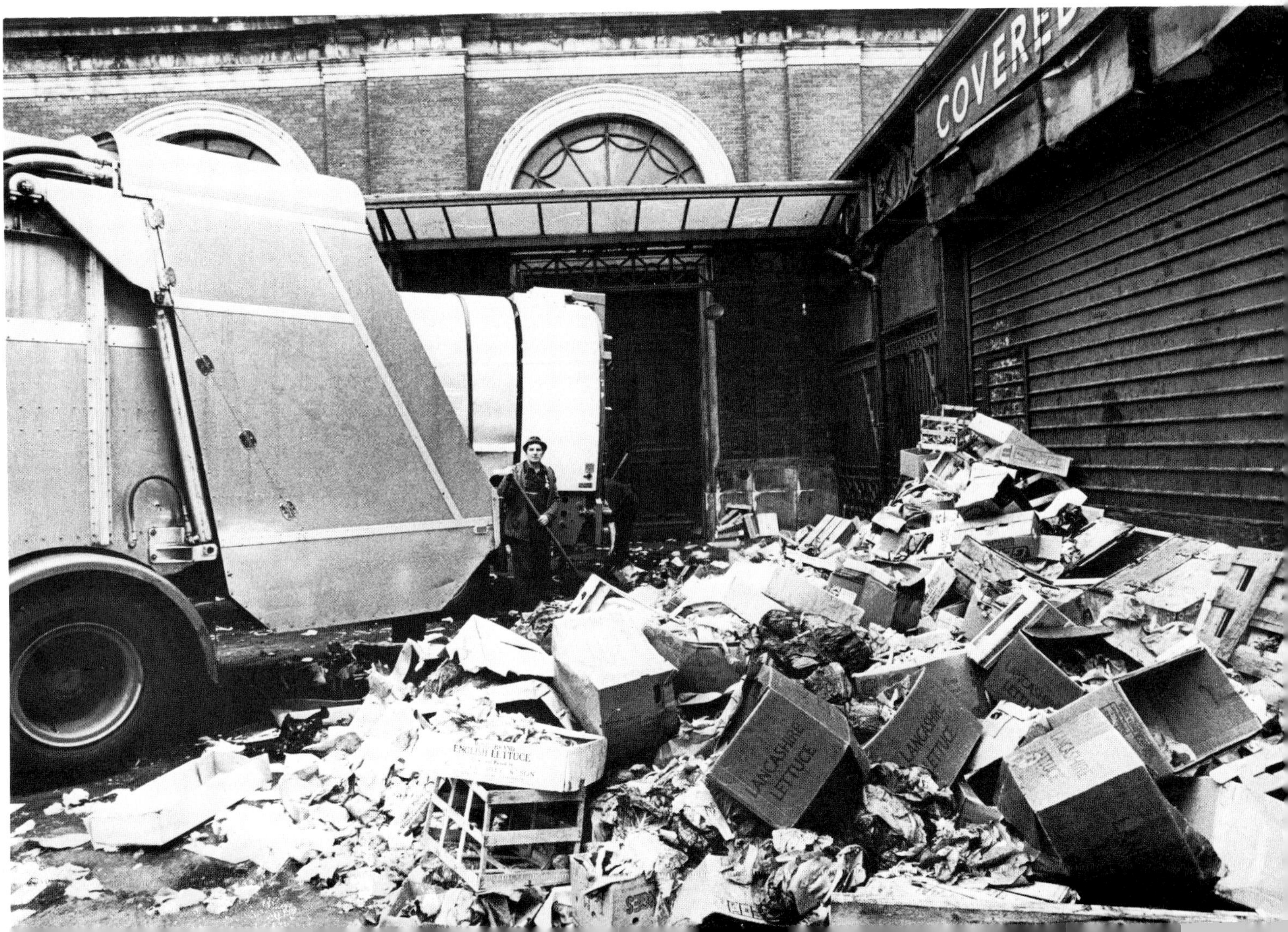

COVERED
LANCASHIRE
LETTUCE
ENGLISH LETTUCE

A message from the Chairman of the Covent Garden Market
Authority, Sir Henry Hardman, K.C.B.

In November 1974 old Covent Garden Market reached the end of
the road. After more than three centuries of trading, the out-of-date
buildings in congested streets involving inefficient handling
techniques have been replaced by modern methods of wholesale
distribution. In its 68-acre home at Vauxhall, 2½ miles away on the
south side of the river, New Covent Garden Market is already
proving that this historic move was more than worthwhile. Turn-
round times for vehicles are much faster; there has been a
substantial reduction in wastage; and the consumer is being supplied
with fresher produce. The new market, designed for 20th century
conditions, offers splendid opportunities. Whilst we may look back
with nostalgia at the passing of the old market, we look forward also
with pride and enthusiasm to ensuring that in its new home Covent
Garden Market's reputation for quality and service goes on growing.

Saphir
D 50
D 49 Saphir
D 48
D 47
D 46
D 45
Look for the label on OUTSPAN quality lemons.
O·K
GUERNSEY TOMS
GUERNSEY TOM
PASCUAL HERMANOS, S.A.
Vauxhall

# Acknowledgements

I wish to thank the Covent Garden Market Authority
and all the people in Covent Garden Market who made
my early mornings so enjoyable.

To N